T0087585

BOOTS RANDOLPH
some favorite songs

❧ • ❧

B♭ TENOR SAXOPHONE/TRUMPET

E♭ ALTO SAXOPHONE

To access audio visit:
www.halleonard.com/mylibrary

3308-8335-1349-6526

ISBN 978-1-59615-744-6

Music Minus One

EXCLUSIVELY DISTRIBUTED BY

HAL•LEONARD®

7777 W. BLUEMOUND RD. P.O. BOX 13819 MILWAUKEE, WI 53213

Visit Hal Leonard Online at
www.halleonard.com

From the Producer . . .

I feel very blessed to have known Boots Randolph for twenty-five years. I first met him when my father, the late comedian Ralph Smith, was recording a comedy album at Boots' legendary Printer's Alley nightclub in 1980. I remember being blown away by Boots and his band. Later that year Fred Foster hired me to play bass on Boots' last project for Monument Records, *Dedication*. Fast forward to 1996 – I had just moved back to Nashville after a stint in France. An opportunity to "sub" on Boots' band one night led to him offering me the job full-time, and I have no intention of ever leaving! I have had the pleasure of producing several records on Boots through the last ten years, and this latest offering is something truly special for all of us involved in the making of it. Through the years, Boots has always had a "concept" in mind when he began a new project. Together, we have done a project of Nashville classic recordings, a Christmas project, and a gospel project. Boots and I had talked many late nights driving back to Nashville about a new project – we just never seemed to come up with a concept that we were as enthused about after a good night's sleep. One day driving to Boots' home to talk about recording, it hit me. Boots is 78 years old, he has cut nearly fifty albums, he is playing as well as he has ever played – who needs a concept? Let's just record a group of Boots' favorite songs, songs he had never recorded previously. Well, there's a concept for you.

We discussed a few titles, and made plans to get together at the studio on a Saturday to "see if anything would happen." Well, did it ever. The first session opened a floodgate, and we soon had fourteen songs that we really wanted to record – and that's what we did. Boots is fond of calling great standards "evergreens," and that is a wonderful description of the titles represented here. It seems like the last few years have produced a glut of artists recording the great standards, so what could we bring to the table that would be new and unique? The answer is in the artist himself. Boots is one of the most unique instrumentalists in the history of modern music. He has proven to be a special interpreter of great melodies. He has proven to be a master of the saxophone in many genres, from country to blues, to pop, to swinging jazz. He possesses one of the most imitated and respected "tones" in the business. On every song in this collection, you will hear a master musician deliver the melody in a way that only Boots can, and you will hear the most adventurous solos that Boots has recorded to date. His legion of fans will get a huge dose of Boots' horn on this project, with no apologies. Our drummer, Ray Von Rotz, repeatedly reminded us all that we didn't need to cheat the boss out of any choruses on these songs, and I am so thrilled that we didn't. We tackled some very difficult music, both harmonically and technically. On *Take Me Out to the Ballgame* it is Boots that burns up a couple of choruses – first take, I might add – while the rest of us burned some serious calories trying to stay in the same "ballpark" as Boots.

I want to mention a very special song: our title cut. I don't think I have ever heard a fan talk to Boots without asking him if he has a favorite sax player. They want to know who his influences are, and why he became the sax player he is today. Boots always mentions the huge names in the jazz sax world, players like Ben Webster, Coleman Hawkins, Lester Young, and Charlie Parker. However, he never fails to mention a man named Don Byas. I had heard Byas mentioned by a lot of jazz experts, but was not too familiar with his work. As we started picking material for this project, Boots brought me a copy of Don Byas playing a great old song called *Candy*. I was floored. First of all, Byas plays the song brilliantly. His time is incredible. His note choice is flawless. His tone is incredibly "contemporary" for his time period. And as a huge fan of Boots, I suddenly put part of the puzzle together. A great musician is a product of his influences, and with his own stamp of creativity becomes a unique artist. Well, thank you, Mr. Byas, for what you brought to the table! I have been lucky enough to have worked with and become friends of many of the top sax players in music today. Bill Evans, the great sax player from Miles Davis's 1980's supergroups came to Nashville to do a record. We have been friends for many years, and he knew that I was working with Boots. He asked if Boots would come in and do a duet with him. One of the first sax players his parents exposed him to at a young age was Boots, and he has been a huge fan for many years. We had great fun making that duet. Kirk Whalum might possibly be the most respected tenor sax player in the current crop of jazz stars. He is a good friend of mine, and has actually told me that one of the reasons he made the move to Nashville years back was "to breathe the same air that Boots did." So, in the same way that these young musicians revere Boots, Boots is giving something back on this record. Boots loves these songs and this is his gift to the listeners.

The band on this record is very special, too. Ray Von Rotz has been with Boots well over twenty years. A great musician, and versatile drummer, Ray found his niche with Boots. Nobody plays this material like Ray. He never ceases to be musical at any tempo or style. Steve Willets joined the band five years ago, and what a find he turned out to be. Steve is not only a tremendous pianist, but he is a fabulous singer, and an encyclopedia of the jazz idiom. He brings incredible energy to the stage and studio. His "time" is just wonderful and he is a great arranger. Roddy Smith is the guitarist on the project. He has been on several of Boots' projects in the past, and began performing live with the group earlier this year. He plays great tasty rhythm as well as some beautiful, bluesy, soulful solos on the record. I played the bass on the record, as I also do on Boots' live shows. His music never ceases to challenge me. I have to admit, I spend most of my time playing Boots' music with a smile on my face. I know that working with him is the highest honor I could have as a player. He always brings his "A game," as Tiger Woods says. He is a true example of being a pro musician. We can't wait to start the next record!

- *Tim Smith*

4275

CONTENTS

B♭ TENOR SAXOPHONE/TRUMPET

Bb Instrument

I'm Beginning to See the Light

Don George, Johnny Hodges,
Duke Ellington and Harry James

I'm Beginning To See The Light
Featured in SOPHISTICATED LADIES
Words and Music by Don George, Johnny Hodges, Duke Ellington and Harry James
Copyright © 1944 (Renewed 1971) by Famous Music LLC in the USA
This arrangement Copyright © 2007 by Famous Music LLC in the USA
Rights for the world outside of the U.S.A. Controlled by Chappell & Co.
International Copyright Secured. All Rights Reserved.

B♭ Instrument

Billie's Bounce

♩ = 140

Charlie Parker

Bb Instrument

Bb Instrument

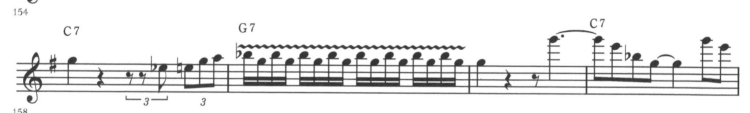

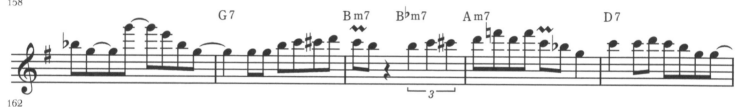

I'll Be Seeing You

Words and Music by
Sammy Fain and Irving Kahal

MMO 4275

Take Me Out to the Ballgame

Words and Music by
Jack Norwoth and Albert von Tilzer

MMO 4275

B♭ Instrument

Candy

Words and Music by
Alex Kramer, Joan Whitney and Mack David

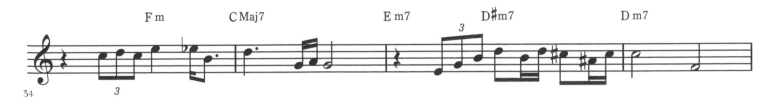

Bb Instrument

Basically Blues

Phil Wilson

Bb Instrument

Bb Instrument

'Round Midnight

Words by Bernie Hanighen
Music by Thelonious Monk and Cootie Williams

Dream Dancing

Cole Porter

Eb ALTO SAXOPHONE

Eb Instrument

I'm Beginning to See the Light

Words and Music by
Don George, Johnny Hodges,
Duke Ellington and Harry James

Billie's Bounce

♩ = 140

Charlie Parker

30

E♭ Instrument

I'll Be Seeing You

Words and Music by
Sammy Fain and Irving Kahal

Eb Instrument

Take Me Out to the Ballgame

Words and Music by
Jack Norwoth and Albert von Tilzer

Eb Alto Sax

Eb Instrument

Candy

Words and Music by
Alex Kramer, Joan Whitney and Mack David

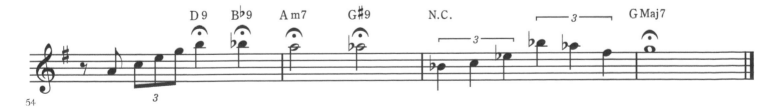

Basically Blues

Phil Wilson

Guitar/Piano solo

46

(74-119)

MMO 4275

Eb Instrument

Eb Instrument

'Round Midnight

Words by Bernie Hanighen
Music by Thelonious Monk and Cootie Williams

Dream Dancing

Words and Music by
Cole Porter

Eb Instrument